STEP-BY-STEP

Cooking for One & Two

STEP-BY-STEP

Cooking for One & Two

ROSEMARY WADEY

SHOOTING STAR PRESS

This edition printed in 1995 for:
Shooting Star Press Inc
230 Fifth Avenue – Suite 1212
New York, NY 10001

Shooting Star Press books are available at special discounts for bulk purchases for sales promotions,
premiums, fund-raising, or educational use. Special edition or book excerpts can also be created to
specification. For details contact: Special Sales Director, Shooting Star Press Inc.,
230 Fifth Avenue, Suite 1212, New York, NY 10001

ISBN 1 57335 008 7

Produced by Haldane Mason, London

Printed in Italy

Acknowledgements:
Art Direction: Ron Samuels
Editor: Joanna Swinnerton
Series Design: Pedro & Frances Prá-Lopez/Kingfisher Design
Page Design: Somewhere Creative
Photography: Joff Lee
Styling: John Lee Studios
Home Economist: Rosemary Wadey

Photographs on pages 6, 18, 34, 48 & 62 reproduced by permission of
ZEFA Picture Library (UK) Ltd.

Note:
Unless otherwise stated, milk is assumed to be full-fat, eggs are AA large
and pepper is freshly ground black pepper.

Contents

CHAPTER ONE

Soups & Appetizers

Soups and appetizers can easily be served as light meals and snacks too, a very important part of cooking for only one or two people. But having said that, it is essential that you always prepare, cook and serve proper meals, whether you are on your own, in a twosome or part of a large family; these soups and appetizers are filling, nutritious, and easy to make. The soups in particular can be made in large quantities to serve over two or three days, or frozen for future use, which will save you from spending too much time in the kitchen.

When it comes to planning an elegant meal for two, the recipes here cover a wide range of tastes, and suggest slightly different ways of serving old favorites. Soups are always popular; the blend of nectarines with peppered Camembert conjures up a new taste; smoked salmon pâté complements an avocado beautifully; and a vegetarian cheese pâté will suit all tastes.

Opposite: A simple soup makes an excellent meal for one or two people; it is easy to prepare and satisfying to eat.

STEP 1

STEP 2

STEP 3

STEP 4

CHICKEN & CORN CHOWDER

A quick and satisfying soup, full of flavor and different textures. This will serve two people for one day or one person for two days.

SERVES 2

2 tsp oil
1 tbsp butter or margarine
1 small onion, chopped finely
1 chicken leg quarter or 2–3 drumsticks
1 tbsp all-purpose flour
2½ cups chicken stock
½ small red, yellow or orange bell pepper,
    seeded and finely chopped
2 large tomatoes, peeled and chopped
2 tsp tomato paste
8-ounce can corn, drained
generous pinch of dried oregano
¼ tsp ground coriander
salt and pepper
chopped fresh parsley to garnish

1 Heat the oil and butter or margarine in a saucepan, and fry the onion slowly until beginning to soften. Cut the chicken quarter, if using, into 2 pieces. Add the chicken to the saucepan, and fry until golden-brown all over.

2 Add the flour, and cook for 1–2 minutes. Then add the stock gradually. Bring to a boil, and simmer for 5 minutes.

3 Add the bell pepper, tomatoes, tomato paste, corn, oregano, coriander, and seasoning. Cover and simmer slowly for about 20 minutes until the chicken is very tender.

4 Remove the chicken from the soup. Strip off the flesh, and chop finely. Return the chopped meat to the soup.

5 Adjust the seasoning, and simmer for an additional 2–3 minutes before sprinkling with parsley and serving very hot with crusty bread.

NOTE

If preferred, the chicken may be removed from the soup when tender to serve separately.

STEP 1

STEP 2

STEP 4

STEP 5

LEEK, POTATO & CARROT SOUP

A quick chunky soup, ideal for a snack or a quick lunch. The leftovers can be puréed to make one portion of creamed soup for the next day.

SERVES 2

1 leek, about 6 ounces
1 tbsp oil
1 garlic clove, crushed
3 cups chicken or vegetable stock
1 bay leaf
$\frac{1}{4}$ tsp ground cumin
1 cup diced potatoes
1 cup coarsely grated carrot
salt and pepper
chopped fresh parsley to garnish

PUREED SOUP:
5–6 tbsp milk
1–2 tbsp heavy cream, crème fraîche or sour
   cream

1 Trim off some of the coarse green part of the leek. Then slice thinly, and rinse in cold water. Drain well.

2 Heat the oil in a saucepan. Add the leek and garlic, and fry slowly for 2–3 minutes until soft but barely colored. Add the stock, bay leaf, cumin, and seasoning, and bring to a boil.

3 Add the diced potato to the saucepan. Cover and simmer slowly for 10–15 minutes until the potato is just tender but not broken up.

4 Add the grated carrot and simmer for an additional 2–3 minutes. Adjust the seasoning. Discard the bay leaf, and serve sprinkled liberally with chopped parsley.

5 To make a puréed soup, first purée the leftovers (about half the original soup) in a blender or food processor, or press through a strainer until smooth, and then return to a clean saucepan with the milk. Bring to a boil, and simmer for 2–3 minutes. Adjust the seasoning, and stir in the cream or crème fraîche before serving sprinkled with chopped parsley.

HELPFUL HINT

If you make double quantities of this soup, half can be frozen to use at a later date.

STEP 1

STEP 3

STEP 5

STEP 6

SMOKED SALMON PATE WITH AVOCADO

Use trimmings of smoked salmon blended with hard-cooked egg and soft cheese to serve garnished with slices of avocado and tomatoes for an elegant appetizer for two or main dish for one.

SERVES 1–2

2 ounces smoked salmon pieces
1 hard-cooked egg
3 tbsp low-fat soft cheese
1 small garlic clove, crushed (optional)
1 tsp lemon or lime juice
about 2 tbsp natural fromage frais or
  natural yogurt
1–2 tomatoes
1 ripe avocado
1 tbsp French dressing (see page 38)
pepper
watercress to garnish

1 Put the pieces of smoked salmon into a food processor, and process until finely chopped. Alternatively, chop the smoked salmon very finely.

2 Add the hard-cooked egg, and continue processing until well chopped and blended. Then add the soft cheese, garlic, lemon or lime juice, and pepper. Continue processing until well blended. Alternatively, grate the egg finely into the other ingredients, and mix.

3 Add sufficient fromage frais or yogurt to give a piping consistency, and place in a pastry bag fitted with a large star tip. Chill until needed.

4 Halve the tomatoes, and cut into thin wedges. Halve the avocado. Peel carefully, and remove the pit. Cut each avocado half into a fan by slicing from the round end to the narrow stem end but leaving a "hinge."

5 Spread out the avocado fan on a small plate, interleaving the tomato wedges with the avocado slices.

6 Pipe or spoon a whirl of smoked salmon pâté at the stem end of the avocado fan.

7 Spoon a little French dressing over each tomato and avocado fan. Garnish with watercress and serve with crackers, toast or crusty bread.

VARIATIONS

Smoked mackerel or kippers may be used for the pâté instead of smoked salmon. The pâté may also be piped to fill the cavities of avocado halves.

STEP 1

STEP 2

STEP 3

STEP 5

PEPPERED CAMEMBERT & NECTARINE SALAD

An unusual blend of flavors and textures, but one that certainly whets the appetite.

SERVES 1

1–2 × 1-ounce portions Camembert cheese
1 tbsp coarse steak pepper
1–2 nectarines
1¹/₂-in. piece cucumber
1 tbsp pecan halves or cashew nuts
mixed salad greens

DRESSING:
1 tbsp sesame oil
1 tsp balsamic vinegar
generous pinch of dry mustard
pinch of sugar
1 garlic clove, crushed (optional)
salt and pepper

1 Cut the rind off the Camembert cheese. Cut the cheese into cubes or slices, and roll in the coarse pepper. Chill.

2 Halve the nectarines. Remove the pit, and slice thinly. Put into a bowl.

3 Cut the cucumber into dice or thin narrow sticks, and add to the nectarines with the nuts.

4 Whisk all the ingredients for the dressing together, adding seasoning to taste, and pour over the nectarine salad; toss lightly.

5 Arrange a few mixed salad greens on a serving plate, and spoon the salad on top.

6 Arrange the peppered Camembert on the salad, and serve with crusty bread or rolls.

VARIATIONS

Brie may be used instead of Camembert, and peaches can be used in place of the nectarines, if you prefer.

14

STEP 1

STEP 2

STEP 3

STEP 4

WALNUT, EGG & CHEESE PATE

This unusual mixture, flavored with parsley and dill, can be served as a pâté with crackers, crusty bread, or toast, or used as a stuffing for tomatoes, celery, or other vegetables.

SERVES 2

1 celery stalk
1–2 scallions, trimmed
¼ cup shelled walnuts
1 tbsp chopped fresh parsley
1 tsp chopped fresh dill or ½ tsp dried
   dillweed
1 garlic clove, crushed
generous dash Worcestershire sauce
½ cup cottage cheese
½ cup blue cheese, such as Stilton or Danish
   Blue
1 hard-cooked egg
2 tbsp butter
salt and pepper
fresh herbs to garnish

1 Chop the celery finely. Slice the scallions very finely. Chop the walnuts evenly but not too finely. Place in a bowl.

2 Add the chopped herbs, garlic, and Worcestershire sauce, and mix well. Then stir the cottage cheese evenly through the mixture.

3 Grate the blue cheese and hard-cooked egg finely into the mixture, and season to taste.

4 Melt the butter, and stir through the pâté. Then spoon into one serving dish or two individual dishes, but do not press down firmly. Chill until set.

5 Garnish with fresh herbs, and serve with crackers, toast, or fresh, crusty bread, and a few crudités, if liked.

STUFFING

To use as a stuffing, cut the tops off extra-large tomatoes, and scoop out the seeds. Fill with the pâté, piling it up, or spoon into the hollows of celery stalks cut into 2-in. pieces.

CHAPTER TWO

Snacks & Quick Meals

Being able to prepare food quickly can be very important in our busy lives, as we often need a quick meal or snack during the day or before going out, but have limited time in which to make it. No one wants to spend too much time in the kitchen, so the following recipes have been devised with speed in mind, and they cater for all tastes and times of day as well as for individuals and couples.

With a little imagination, a quick meal can be just as satisfying as any other meal. A pasta and tuna fish layer can be varied by using cooked chicken or other cold meats, or vegetables in a savory sauce; quiches are just as good hot as cold; croquettes can use up any type of cooked meat for a really tasty snack with a mixture of stir-fried vegetables; and corn and potato fritters double up well for breakfast (perhaps with bacon or sausages), brunch or an anytime snack.

Opposite: *Dried pasta is a particularly useful ingredient for meals for one or two. It will keep in your kitchen cupboard for a considerable time, can be bought in a wide variety of shapes and flavors, and is quick and easy to cook.*

STEP 2

STEP 4

STEP 5

STEP 6

SPINACH FILO BASKETS

If you use frozen spinach, it only needs to be defrosted and drained before being mixed with the cheeses and seasonings. Filo pastry can be defrosted sufficiently to remove the four sheets of pastry you need, then returned to the freezer to use at a later date.

MAKES 2

3 cups fresh leaf spinach, washed and
    chopped roughly, or ¹/₂ cup defrosted
    frozen spinach
2–4 scallions, trimmed and chopped, or
    1 tbsp finely chopped onion
1 garlic clove, crushed
2 tbsp grated Parmesan cheese
³/₄ cup grated sharp Cheddar cheese
large pinch of ground allspice
1 egg yolk
4 sheets filo pastry
2 tbsp melted butter
salt and pepper
2 scallions to garnish

1 If using fresh spinach, cook it in the minimum of boiling salted water for 3–4 minutes until tender. Drain very thoroughly, using a potato masher to remove excess liquid. Then chop and put into a bowl. If using frozen spinach, simply drain and chop.

2 Add the scallions or onion, garlic, cheeses, allspice, egg yolk and seasoning, and mix well.

3 Grease 2 individual muffin pans, or ovenproof dishes or pans about 5 in. in diameter, and 1¹/₂ in. deep. Cut

the filo pastry sheets in half to make 8 pieces, and brush each lightly with melted butter.

4 Place one piece of filo pastry in a pan or dish, and then cover with a second piece at right angles to the first. Add two more pieces at right angles, so that all the corners are in different places. Line the other pan in the same way.

5 Spoon the spinach mixture into the "baskets" and place in a preheated oven at 350°F for about 20 minutes, or until the pastry is golden-brown. Garnish with a scallion tassel, and serve hot or cold.

6 Make scallion tassels about 30 minutes before required. Trim off the root end, and cut to a length of 2–3 in. Make a series of cuts from the green end to within ³/₄ in. of the other end. Place in a bowl of ice water to open out. Drain well before use.

STEP 3

STEP 4

STEP 5

STEP 6

ZUCCHINI, TARRAGON & BACON QUICHES

Individual pastry shells with a filling of grated zucchini, fresh tarragon and crispy bacon in a fromage frais custard to serve hot or cold.

MAKES 2

DOUGH:
$^{3}/_{4}$ cup all-purpose flour
pinch of salt
3 tbsp butter or block margarine

FILLING:
1 small zucchini, about 3 ounces
4 slices lean bacon, diced
1 scallion, trimmed and chopped
$^{1}/_{4}$ tsp chopped fresh tarragon or generous
   pinch of dried tarragon
1 egg
6 tbsp natural fromage frais
1–2 tsp grated Parmesan cheese
salt and pepper

1 To make the dough, sift the flour and salt into a bowl, and rub in the butter or margarine until the mixture resembles fine bread crumbs. Add sufficient cold water to mix to a pliable dough, and knead very lightly. Then wrap the dough in plastic wrap, and chill while preparing the filling.

2 Trim the zucchini and grate coarsely into a bowl. Cover with boiling water, and leave for 5 minutes. Drain very thoroughly, using a potato masher if necessary to extract the water.

3 Fry the bacon in its own fat until well sealed, then add to the zucchini with the scallion and tarragon.

4 Roll out the dough and use to line 2 individual fluted quiche pans about $4^{1}/_{2}$ in. in diameter.

5 Divide the zucchini mixture between the 2 pans. Beat the egg with the fromage frais, and season well.

6 Pour the custard into the pie shells, and sprinkle with the cheese. Place in a preheated oven at 400°F for 25–30 minutes, or until the custard is set firm and the pastry is cooked through. Serve hot or cold. The quiches can be frozen for up to 2 months.

STEP 2

STEP 3

STEP 4

STEP 5

CORN & POTATO FRITTERS

An ideal supper dish for two, or for one if you halve the quantities. You can use the remaining corn in another recipe.

SERVES 2

2 tbsp oil
1 small onion, sliced thinly
1 garlic clove, crushed
12 ounces potatoes
8-ounce can corn, drained
$\frac{1}{2}$ tsp dried oregano
1 egg, beaten
$\frac{1}{2}$ cup grated Edam or Gouda cheese
salt and pepper
2–4 eggs
2–4 tomatoes, sliced
parsley sprigs, to garnish

1 Heat 1 tablespoon of the oil in a nonstick skillet. Add the onion and garlic, and fry very slowly until soft, but only lightly colored, stirring frequently. Remove from the heat.

2 Grate the potatoes coarsely into a bowl, and mix in the corn, oregano, beaten egg, and seasoning; then add the fried onion.

3 Heat the remaining oil in the skillet. Divide the potato mixture in half, and add to the pan to make 2 oval-shaped cakes, leveling and shaping the cakes with a spatula.

4 Cook slowly for about 10 minutes until browned underneath and almost cooked through, keeping in shape with the spatula and loosening so the fritters don't stick.

5 Sprinkle each potato fritter with the grated cheese, and place under a preheated moderately hot broiler until golden-brown.

6 Meanwhile, poach either 1 or 2 eggs for each person until just cooked. Transfer the fritters to warmed plates, and top each with the eggs and sliced tomatoes. Garnish with parsley, and serve at once.

CHICKEN & ALMOND CROQUETTES WITH STIR-FRIED VEGETABLES

Cooked potatoes and cooked chicken are combined to make tasty croquettes rolled in chopped almonds to serve with stir-fried vegetables.

STEP 1

SERVES 1

4 ounces boiled potatoes
3 ounces carrots
1 cup cooked chicken meat
1 garlic clove, crushed
$\frac{1}{2}$ tsp dried tarragon or thyme
generous pinch of ground allspice or
    coriander
1 egg yolk, or $\frac{1}{2}$ egg, beaten
about $\frac{1}{4}$ cup slivered almonds
salt and pepper

STIR-FRIED VEGETABLES:
1 celery stalk
2 scallions, trimmed
1 tbsp oil
8 baby corn cobs
about 10–12 snow peas or sugar snap peas,
    trimmed
2 tsp balsamic vinegar

1 Grate the boiled potatoes and raw carrots coarsely into a bowl. Chop finely or grind the chicken, and add to the vegetables with the garlic, tarragon or thyme, allspice or coriander and plenty of seasoning.

2 Add the egg yolk or beaten egg, and bind the ingredients together.

3 Divide the mixture in half, and shape each into a sausage.

4 Chop the almonds evenly, and then roll each croquette in the nuts until evenly coated. Either place in a greased ovenproof dish, and cook in a preheated oven at 400°F for about 20 minutes, or until lightly browned; or fry in a little oil until browned all over and cooked through.

5 While the croquettes cook, prepare the vegetables. Cut the celery and scallions into narrow slanting slices. Heat the oil in a skillet and toss in these vegetables. Cook over a high heat for 1–2 minutes. Then add the corn cobs and peas, and cook for 2–3 minutes. Finally, add the vinegar and seasoning to taste.

6 Spoon the stir-fried vegetables on to a serving plate, and place the croquettes beside them. Serve at once.

STEP 3

STEP 4

LEFTOVERS

Any leftover cooked meat or poultry can be used for this dish.

STEP 5

STEP 2

STEP 3

STEP 4

STEP 5

MACARONI & TUNA FISH LAYER

A layer of tuna fish with garlic, mushrooms, and red bell pepper is sandwiched between two layers of macaroni with a crunchy topping.

SERVES 2

1¼ cup dried macaroni
2 tbsp oil
1 garlic clove, crushed
¾ cup sliced button mushrooms
½ red bell pepper, thinly sliced
7-ounce can tuna fish in brine, drained and
    flaked
½ tsp dried oregano
2 tbsp butter or margarine
1 tbsp all-purpose flour
1 cup milk
2 tomatoes, sliced
2 tbsp dried bread crumbs
¼ cup grated sharp Cheddar or Parmesan
    cheese
salt and pepper

1 Cook the macaroni in boiling salted water, with 1 tablespoon of the oil added, until tender, about 12 minutes. Drain, rinse and drain thoroughly.

2 Heat the remaining oil in a saucepan or skillet and fry the garlic, mushrooms, and bell pepper until soft. Add the tuna fish, oregano, and seasoning, and heat through.

3 Grease an ovenproof dish (about 4-cup capacity), and add half the cooked macaroni. Cover with the tuna mixture, and then add the remaining macaroni.

4 To make the sauce, melt the butter or margarine in a saucepan, and stir in the flour. Cook for 1 minute. Add the milk gradually, and bring to a boil. Simmer for a minute or so, stirring continuously, until thickened. Season to taste. Pour the sauce over the macaroni.

5 Lay the sliced tomatoes over the sauce, and sprinkle with the bread crumbs and cheese.

6 Place in a preheated oven at 400°F for about 25 minutes, or until piping hot and the top is well browned.

VARIATIONS

Ring the changes by replacing the tuna fish with chopped cooked chicken, beef, pork or ham, or with 3–4 sliced hard-cooked eggs.

STEP 2

STEP 3

STEP 5

STEP 6

EGGPLANT WITH RISOTTO STUFFING

An eggplant is halved and filled with a risotto mixture, topped with cheese, and baked to make a snack or quick meal for two, or an accompaniment to a main dish.

SERVES 2

¼ cup mixed long-grain and wild rice
1 eggplant, about 12 ounces
1 tbsp olive oil
1 small onion, finely chopped
1 garlic clove, crushed
½ small red bell pepper, cored, deseeded and
    chopped
2 tbsp water
3 tbsp raisins
¼ cup roughly chopped cashew nuts
½ tsp dried oregano
⅓ cup grated sharp Cheddar or Parmesan
    cheese,
salt and pepper
fresh oregano or parsley to garnish

1 Cook the rice in boiling salted water until just tender, about 15 minutes. Drain, rinse and drain again.

2 Bring a large saucepan of water to a boil. Cut the stem off the eggplant, and then cut in half lengthwise. Cut out the flesh from the center carefully, leaving about a ½ in. shell. Blanch the shells in the boiling water for 3–4 minutes. Drain thoroughly.

3 Chop the eggplant flesh finely. Heat the oil in a saucepan or skillet and fry the onion and garlic slowly until beginning to soften. Then add the bell pepper and eggplant flesh, and continue cooking for a couple of minutes before adding the water and cooking for an additional 2–3 minutes.

4 Stir the raisins, cashew nuts, oregano and rice into the eggplant mixture, and season well with salt and pepper.

5 Lay the eggplant shells in an ovenproof dish, and spoon in the rice mixture, piling it up well. Cover and place in a preheated oven at 375°F for 20 minutes.

6 Remove the lid, and sprinkle the cheese over the rice. Place under a preheated moderate broiler for 3–4 minutes until golden-brown. Serve hot garnished with oregano or parsley.

STEP 3

STEP 4

STEP 5

STEP 6

BROCCOLI WITH FLUFFY EGGS

Broccoli or cauliflower florets in a mustard sauce are topped with an egg yolk set in beaten egg white and finished off with grated cheese.

SERVES 1

1½ cups trimmed broccoli or cauliflower
  florets
1 tbsp butter or margarine
2 tbsp all-purpose flour
⅔ cup milk
1 tbsp coarse grain mustard
squeeze of lemon juice
¾ cup grated sharp Cheddar cheese,
1 large egg, separated
salt and pepper
paprika to garnish

1 Cook the broccoli or cauliflower in boiling salted water until tender but still crisp, about 3–4 minutes.

2 Meanwhile, melt the butter or margarine in a small saucepan. Stir in the flour, and cook for a minute or so. Add the milk gradually, stirring continuously, and bring to a boil until thickened. Season well, and stir in the mustard and lemon juice. Simmer for 1–2 minutes.

3 Remove the sauce from the heat, and stir in two-thirds of the cheese until melted.

4 Drain the broccoli or cauliflower very thoroughly, and place on an ovenproof plate or dish. Pour the sauce over the vegetables.

5 Beat the egg white until very stiff, and season lightly. Pile the egg white on top of the broccoli or cauliflower, and make a well in the center.

6 Drop the egg yolk into the well in the egg white, and sprinkle with the remaining cheese. Place under a preheated moderate broiler for 3–4 minutes until the meringue is lightly browned and the cheese melted. Serve sprinkled with paprika.

VARIATIONS

The fluffy eggs can be served on a variety of other vegetables with or without a sauce, or on poached haddock.

CHAPTER THREE

Two-day Meals & Snacks

When you are on your own, the task of cooking for just one or two can become a little tedious. Such small quantities usually take less time to prepare, but the cooking time is the same as for several people, so it is often a good idea to cook sufficient for two days. Alternatively, you can cook two portions of the main ingredient, such as chicken pieces or a tomato sauce, and set aside one portion, ready to be turned into a different meal the following day. The recipes in this section are devised with both of these possibilities in mind, including two salads which will improve with keeping overnight in the refrigerator.

For example, if you like salmon, simply poach two portions and serve one with a sauce on one day, and make the other into kedgeree the next; cook some ground beef with spices, and then transform half of it into a creamy curry to serve with poppadoms and chutney; serve roast chicken thighs with a crunchy topping, then use half of the meat to make a spicy chicken salad, served with rice.

Many supermarkets are good at providing single and small portions of meat and fish. Small fish, chops and cutlets are ideal for meals for one or two. It takes only a little imagination to conjure up lots of new ideas, even if you are cooking small quantities.

Opposite: Use as wide a range of ingredients as you can, and use the freshest fruits and vegetables available to ensure that your meals are varied and full of flavor.

STEP 1

STEP 2

STEP 4

STEP 6

SALMON WITH AVOCADO & TARRAGON SAUCE/KEDGEREE

Two salmon cutlets or fillets are cooked at the same time, one to serve with a delicious avocado sauce, and the other to be made into a kedgeree the next day.

SERVES 1

2 × 6-ounce salmon cutlets or fillets
butter
1 bay leaf
1 tsp lemon juice
salt and pepper

SAUCE:
¹/₂ ripe avocado
1 tsp lemon juice
2 tbsp sour cream or natural fromage frais
1 scallion, trimmed and chopped finely, or
*   1¹/₂ tsp chopped chives*
1 tsp chopped fresh tarragon or ¹/₂ tsp dried

SALMON KEDGEREE:
¹/₄ cup long-grain rice
1 tbsp butter or margarine
1 small onion, sliced thinly
1 garlic clove, crushed
1 tsp chopped fresh tarragon or 2 tsp
*   chopped fresh parsley*
1 hard-cooked egg, chopped
2 tbsp sour cream or natural fromage frais
salt and pepper

1 Season the salmon. Lightly butter a sheet of foil large enough to enclose the fish, and place the salmon on it. Add the bay leaf and lemon juice, and seal the edges of the package of foil firmly.

2 Place the package in a saucepan, and cover with cold water. Bring to a boil. Cover and simmer for 10 minutes. Remove from the heat, and leave for 5 minutes. Remove from the pan.

3 To make the sauce, mash the avocado with the lemon juice, then add the sour cream, scallion or chives, tarragon and seasoning, beating until smooth.

4 Remove one salmon piece, and place on a plate. Spoon the avocado sauce around the fish, and serve. Let the other salmon piece cool; then chill and set aside for the kedgeree.

5 To make the kedgeree, cook the rice in boiling salted water for 12–14 minutes, then drain. Remove the skin and bones from the salmon, and flake.

6 Melt the butter or margarine in a saucepan, and fry the onion and garlic slowly until soft. Then add the flaked salmon and cooked rice, and heat through completely, stirring almost continuously. Add the tarragon or parsley, chopped egg, sour cream or fromage frais, and plenty of seasoning, and heat slowly. Serve piping hot.

STEP 1

STEP 2

STEP 3

STEP 4

PASTA MEDLEY

Strips of cooked chicken or pork are tossed with colored pasta in a pesto-flavored dressing with grapes and carrot sticks. This will keep well to be eaten again the next day; if you like, throw in a few new ingredients to change the flavor a little.

SERVES 2

4–5 ounces dried pasta shapes, such as
  twists or bows
1 tbsp oil
1 tbsp French dressing
2 tbsp thick mayonnaise
2 tsp bottled pesto sauce
1 tbsp sour cream or natural fromage frais
6 ounces cooked chicken meat or lean cooked
  pork
1–2 celery stalks
1 cup black grapes (preferably seedless)
1 large carrot, trimmed
salt and pepper
celery leaves to garnish

1 Cook the pasta in boiling salted water with the oil until just tender, about 12 minutes. Drain thoroughly, rinse and drain again. Transfer to a bowl, and mix in the French dressing while hot. Leave until cold.

2 Combine the mayonnaise, pesto sauce and sour cream or fromage frais in a bowl, and season to taste.

3 Cut the chicken or pork into narrow strips. Cut the celery diagonally into narrow slices. Reserve a few grapes for garnish. Halve the rest,

and remove any seeds. Cut the carrot into narrow julienne strips.

4 Add the chicken or pork, celery, halved grapes, carrot, and mayonnaise to the pasta, and toss thoroughly. Adjust the seasoning.

5 Arrange the salad on 2 plates, and garnish with the remaining grapes and celery leaves.

FRENCH DRESSING

You can make your own French dressing by whisking together 1 part wine vinegar to 3 parts olive oil, and seasoning to taste.

VARIATIONS

Other vegetables and fruit that are available can be used to vary the taste of this salad, but make sure the flavors and textures complement each other.

STEP 1

STEP 2

STEP 4

STEP 5

CRUNCHY-TOPPED CHICKEN/ SPICED CHICKEN SALAD

Cook four chicken pieces together, and serve two hot, topped with a crunchy herb mixture and white sauce, accompanied by potatoes or pasta; then turn the remainder into a spicy chicken salad.

SERVES 2

4 chicken thighs
oil for brushing
garlic powder
¹/₂ eating apple, coarsely grated
1¹/₂ tbsp dry parsley and thyme stuffing mix
salt and pepper

SAUCE:
1 tbsp butter or margarine
2 tsp all-purpose flour
5 tbsp milk
2 tbsp dry white wine or stock
¹/₂ tsp dried mustard powder
1 tsp capers or chopped gherkins

SPICED CHICKEN SALAD:
¹/₂ small onion, finely chopped
1 tbsp oil
1 tsp tomato paste
¹/₂ tsp curry powder
1 tsp apricot jam
1 tsp lemon juice
2 tbsp mayonnaise
1 tbsp sour cream or natural fromage frais
³/₄ cup seedless grapes, halved
¹/₄ cup long-grain rice, cooked

1 Place the chicken in an ovenproof dish. Brush with oil. Add garlic powder, and season. Place in a preheated oven at 400°F for 25 minutes, or until almost cooked.

2 Mix the apple with the stuffing. Baste the chicken, and spoon the mixture over 2 of the pieces. Return to the oven until the mixture is brown and the chicken is cooked, about 10 minutes.

3 To make the sauce, melt the fat in a saucepan, and stir in the flour. Cook for 1–2 minutes. Add the milk gradually, then the wine or stock, and bring to a boil. Stir in the mustard, capers or gherkins, and seasoning, and simmer for a minute or so. Serve the 2 pieces of chicken with the crunchy topping with the sauce spooned over and around it.

4 For the salad, fry the onion slowly in the oil until barely colored. Add the tomato paste, curry powder, and jam, and cook for 1 minute. Let cool. Blend in a food processor, or press through a strainer. Beat in the lemon juice, mayonnaise and sour cream or fromage frais. Season.

5 Cut the chicken into strips, and add to the sauce with the grapes. Mix well, and chill for at least 2 hours before serving with rice and a green salad.

ITALIAN TOMATO SAUCE WITH PASTA/OCEAN PIE

Fresh tomatoes make a delicious Italian-style sauce which goes equally well with pasta and bacon or white fish and shrimp to give two totally different dishes.

STEP 1

SERVES 1

1 tbsp olive oil
1 small onion, finely chopped
1–2 cloves garlic, crushed
12 ounces tomatoes, peeled and chopped
2 tsp tomato paste
2 tbsp water
2¹/₂–3 ounces dried pasta shapes
³/₄ cup diced lean bacon
¹/₂ cup sliced mushrooms
1 tbsp chopped fresh parsley or 1 tsp
    chopped fresh cilantro
2 tbsp sour cream or natural fromage frais
    (optional)
salt and pepper

OCEAN PIE:
6 ounces white fish fillet, such as cod
4 tbsp milk
¹/₄ cup peeled shrimp
¹/₂ cup roughly chopped mushrooms
¹/₂ tsp dried tarragon
1 cup mashed potatoes
salt and pepper

1 Heat the oil in a saucepan, and fry the onion and garlic gently until soft. Add the tomatoes, tomato paste, water and seasoning. Bring to a boil. Cover and simmer gently for 10 minutes.

2 Cook the pasta in boiling salted water for about 10 minutes, or until just tender.

3 Heat the bacon slowly in a saucepan until the fat runs. Then add the mushrooms, and continue cooking for 3–4 minutes. Drain off any excess oil, and add half the tomato sauce with the parsley or cilantro, and the sour cream if using. Reheat and serve with the well-drained pasta. Set aside the remaining sauce.

4 To make the Ocean Pie, poach the fish in the milk with seasoning added until tender, about 6–8 minutes; then drain.

5 Heat the tomato sauce with the shrimp, mushrooms and tarragon. Flake the fish, discarding any skin and bones, and add to the sauce. Transfer to an ovenproof dish.

6 Pipe or spread the potatoes over the fish, and place in a preheated oven at 400°F for about 25 minutes, or until golden-brown.

STEP 3

STEP 5

STEP 6

STEP 1

STEP 2

STEP 5

STEP 6

TABBOULEH SALAD

This kind of salad is eaten widely throughout the Middle East. Bulgar wheat is easy to prepare: simply soak it in boiling water before adding a variety of ingredients to make this unusual salad. The flavor improves as it is kept, so it tastes even better on the second day.

SERVES 2

1 cup bulgar wheat
2¹/₂ cups boiling water
1 red bell pepper, halved
3 tbsp olive oil
1 garlic clove, crushed
grated rind of ¹/₂ lime
about 1 tbsp lime juice
1 tbsp chopped fresh mint
1 tbsp chopped fresh parsley
3–4 scallions, trimmed and thinly sliced
8 pitted black olives, halved
¹/₃ cup large salted peanuts or cashew nuts
1–2 tsp lemon juice
2–3 ounces Gruyère cheese
salt and pepper
fresh mint sprigs to garnish

1 Put the bulgar into a bowl, and cover with a boiling water (it should come about 1 in. above the bulgar). Let soak until most of the water has been absorbed, and it is cold – up to an hour.

2 Meanwhile, put the halved red bell pepper, skin-side upward, on a broiler rack, and cook under a preheated moderate broiler until the skin is thoroughly charred. Let cool slightly; then peel off the skin, and discard the seeds. Cut the bell pepper flesh into narrow strips.

3 Whisk together the oil, garlic, lime rind and juice, and seasoning until well blended. Add 1¹/₂ tablespoons of the dressing to the bell peppers, and mix lightly.

4 Drain the soaked bulgar wheat thoroughly, squeezing it in a dry cloth to make it even drier, and place it in a bowl.

5 Add the chopped herbs, scallions, olives, and peanuts or cashew nuts to the bulgar, and toss thoroughly. Add the lemon juice to the remaining dressing, and stir through the salad. Spoon the salad onto one side of 2 serving plates.

6 Cut the cheese into narrow strips, and mix with the bell pepper strips. Spoon alongside the bulgar salad. Garnish with mint sprigs, and serve with warm pocket bread or crusty rolls.

BOBOTIE/CREAMY CURRIED BEEF

Rich savory ground beef is flavored with spices, raisins, tomatoes, and almonds; the next day the leftovers are transformed into a delicious creamy curry.

STEP 1

STEP 2

STEP 3

STEP 5

SERVES 1

1½ cups ground beef
1 onion, chopped
1 garlic clove, crushed
1 large carrot, finely chopped
2 tomatoes, peeled and sliced
2 tsp tomato paste
⅓ cup raisins or golden raisins
⅔ cup beef stock
1½ tbsp wine vinegar
½ tsp ground cumin
¼ tsp ground cinnamon
generous pinch of ground allspice
¼ cup slivered almonds
salt and pepper

CREAMY CURRIED BEEF:
1 tsp medium curry powder
¼ cup long-grain rice
2–3 tbsp sour cream or natural yogurt

TO GARNISH:
1–2 tomatoes
½ small onion
2 poppadoms

1 Put the beef, onion, garlic, and carrot into a saucepan, and heat slowly until the fat runs; then continue until the beef is well sealed.

2 Add the tomatoes, tomato paste, raisins or golden raisins, stock, vinegar, spices, and seasoning, and bring to a boil. Cover and simmer slowly for 20 minutes, until very tender, stirring occasionally.

3 Transfer half the mixture to a bowl, and let cool, then chill. Add the slivered almonds to the remaining beef in the saucepan, and adjust the seasoning. Cook for an additional 2–3 minutes; then serve.

4 The next day, put the beef mixture into a small saucepan, and reheat slowly. Then add the curry powder and a little water if it seems too dry, and simmer for 10 minutes. At the same time, cook the rice in boiling salted water for about 12–14 minutes, or until tender.

5 Stir the sour cream or yogurt into the beef, and reheat slowly. Drain the rice.

6 Slice the tomatoes thinly and the onion very thinly, and mix together. Arrange the rice in a ring on a warmed plate. Spoon the curried beef into the center, and serve with the tomato and onion salad and poppadoms.

CHAPTER FOUR

Main Courses

A meal is usually planned around the main dish, so once you have made your choice, you can then select the vegetable accompaniments. Try to serve potatoes, pasta, or rice with at least one other vegetable; the calorie-conscious can omit the potatoes, and serve two vegetables, one of which should be green. If you are serving an appetizer and a dessert, it is important to choose foods that complement each other. Do not serve two dishes made with pastry, or two dishes which are fried; try to balance a slightly heavier main course with a lighter dessert and vice versa.

When you use the oven, it is economical to cook as much food in it at one time as you can. For instance, put a potato or two in to bake and then add the main dish for the required time. Several vegetables can be cooked together in the same saucepan; ideally you should use a pan with special partitions, but if you don't have one, start off with the vegetable that takes the longest to cook, and then add the rest in turn, according to their cooking time. Drain them together when ready, and serve topped with a knob of butter. If you feel that making a white sauce for just one vegetable portion is extravagant or time-wasting, simply top the vegetable with 1–2 tablespoons of fromage frais, natural yogurt or sour cream – not quite the same as a white sauce but still very good.

Opposite: *Choose a range of different meats and fish to add to your favorite vegetables to create a selection of hearty and satisfying main courses.*

STEP 1

STEP 2

STEP 4

STEP 5

SEAFISH BUNDLES

A mixture of white fish and shellfish in a tangy sauce baked in crisp filo pastry bundles.

SERVES 2

2 tbsp peeled shrimp
8 bottled mussels
6–8 ounces white fish fillets (e.g. cod,
  haddock, flounder), skinned
1/2 cup button mushrooms
1–2 scallions, trimmed
1/2 tsp chopped fresh dill or a large pinch
  dried dillweed
2 tbsp natural fromage frais
1 tbsp thick mayonnaise
6 sheets filo pastry
1 tbsp melted butter or margarine
salt and pepper

SAUCE:
4 tbsp natural fromage frais
2 tbsp thick mayonnaise
pinch of chopped fresh dill or dried dillweed

TO GARNISH:
cooked shrimp in shells (optional)
fresh herbs
lime slices or wedges

1 Put the shrimp into a bowl, halving if large, and then add the mussels. Cut the fish into small cubes; add to the shrimp.

2 Chop the mushrooms, and slice the scallion. Add to the fish with the herbs, fromage frais, mayonnaise, and seasoning. Mix well.

3 Halve each sheet of filo pastry. Place 1 piece on a flat surface, and brush lightly with the melted butter. Cover with another sheet at right angles to the first, and brush again. Then add a third sheet and brush again. Repeat with 3 other piles of filo pastry.

4 Divide the fish mixture evenly between the bundles. Gather the corners of the pastry together carefully, and press together to form a bundle.

5 Place on a greased baking sheet, and brush the pastry with melted fat. Place in a preheated oven at 375°F for about 25 minutes, or until golden-brown and cooked.

6 While the bundles cook, make the sauce. Combine the fromage frais and mayonnaise in a saucepan, and heat slowly, but do not boil. Add the dill and seasoning to taste, and serve with the bundles, garnished with shrimp in their shells, fresh herbs, and lime slices.

STEP 1

STEP 2

STEP 3

STEP 6

SCALLOP & BACON KEBAB

Just for one, this kebab will give a taste of elegance with very little preparation and cooking.

SERVES 1

2 large scallops or 6–8 small scallops
6 slices lean bacon
1 small zucchini, trimmed
1 tsp balsamic vinegar
1 tsp oil
1 tsp lemon juice
generous pinch of dried thyme
pepper

COCONUT RICE:
generous pinch of turmeric
pinch of salt
1 tbsp shredded coconut
¼ cup long-grain rice

TO GARNISH:
watercress
tomato slices

1 If using large scallops, cut each one into 3 pieces. Wrap a slice of bacon around each piece, or around each of the small scallops, if using.

2 Cut the zucchini diagonally into 5 slices. Thread onto a long skewer, alternating with the scallop and bacon rolls.

3 Combine the vinegar, oil, lemon juice, thyme, and pepper, and brush over the kebab. Leave on a plate while cooking the rice.

4 Bring a small saucepan of water to a boil with the turmeric and salt added. Add the coconut and rice, and bring back to a boil. Simmer, uncovered, for 12–14 minutes until tender.

5 Place the kebabs under a preheated moderate broiler for 2–3 minutes on each side until the bacon is crispy and the scallop just cooked.

6 Drain the rice thoroughly, and arrange on a warm serving plate. Place the kebab across the rice, and garnish with watercress and tomato slices.

COQ AU VIN BLANC

Small pieces of chicken are gently simmered with wine, herbs, bacon, mushrooms, and onions to produce a dish reminiscent of a true French meal.

SERVES 2

2 chicken leg quarters
4 thick lean back bacon slices
2 tbsp oil
1 cup pearl onions or 1 large onion, sliced
1 garlic clove, crushed
²/₃ cup dry white wine
1¹/₄ cups chicken stock
1 bay leaf
large pinch of dried oregano
1 tbsp cornstarch
³/₄ cup tiny button mushrooms, trimmed
salt and pepper
chopped fresh parsley to garnish

1 Cut each chicken leg into 2 pieces, and season well. Cut the bacon into ¹/₂-in. strips.

2 Heat the oil in a saucepan. Fry the chicken until golden-brown, and remove from the pan. Add the bacon, onions, and garlic, and fry until lightly browned. Drain off all the fat from the saucepan.

3 Add the wine, stock, bay leaf, oregano and seasoning to the saucepan. Return the chicken, and bring to a boil.

4 Cover the saucepan tightly, and simmer very slowly for about 40–50 minutes, or until the chicken is very tender.

5 Blend the cornstarch with a little cold water, and add to the saucepan with the mushrooms. Bring back to a boil, and simmer for an additional 5 minutes.

6 Adjust the seasoning. Discard the bay leaf, and serve sprinkled liberally with chopped parsley, and with boiled rice or creamed potatoes.

VARIATION

For a traditional Coq au Vin, replace the white wine with red wine, and add 1–2 tablespoons of brandy (if liked) after the cornstarch.

STEP 1

STEP 2

STEP 3

STEP 4

PAN-FRIED LIVER WITH THYME & CAPERS

This elegant dish is very simple to make. You can use either calf's or lamb's liver for the main ingredient.

SERVES 1

*1 slice calf's liver, about 4 ounces, or 2
    smaller slices, or 2 slices lamb's liver
1 tbsp seasoned flour
2 tsp oil
1 tbsp butter or margarine
2 tbsp white wine
$^1\!/_2$ tsp chopped fresh thyme or a large pinch
    of dried thyme
pinch of finely grated lime or lemon rind
2 tsp lemon juice
1 tsp capers
1–2 tbsp heavy cream (optional)
salt and pepper*

*TO GARNISH:
lemon or lime slices
fresh thyme or parsley*

1 Trim the liver if necessary, and toss evenly in the seasoned flour.

2 Heat the oil and butter or margarine in a skillet. When foaming, add the liver and fry for 2–3 minutes on each side, until well sealed and just cooked through. Take care not to overcook or the liver will become tough and hard. Transfer to a plate and keep warm.

3 Add the wine, 1 tablespoon of water, the thyme, citrus rind, lemon juice, capers, and seasoning to the pan juices, and heat through slowly until bubbling and syrupy.

4 If liked, add the cream to the sauce and reheat slowly. Adjust the seasoning and spoon over the liver.

5 Garnish the liver with lemon or lime slices and thyme or parsley, and serve with new potatoes and a salad.

GARNISH

Liver is traditionally served with bacon and onions, and broiled bacon rolls and crisply fried onions can be used as an extra garnish.

STEP 1

STEP 2

STEP 3

STEP 4

NOISETTES OF LAMB WITH SPICY SAUCE

Broiled or fried noisettes of lamb are served on croûtes of fried bread or toast with a spicy tomato and mushroom sauce. Pork noisettes are equally good, if you prefer.

SERVES 2

4 lamb noisettes or cutlets or 4 pork
  noisettes or boneless pork slices
4 × 4-in. rounds of bread
oil or fat for shallow-frying (optional)
fresh herbs to garnish

SAUCE:
6 tbsp red wine
6 tbsp ketchup
2 tbsp water
1 garlic clove, crushed
¾ cup sliced or quartered button
  mushrooms
salt and pepper

1 To make the sauce, put the wine, ketchup, water, and garlic into a saucepan. Bring to a boil, and simmer, uncovered, for 10 minutes until beginning to thicken and evaporate a little. Add seasoning and the mushrooms, and cook for an additional 10 minutes or so, or until the sauce is thick and syrupy, and reduced by at least one third.

2 Meanwhile, prepare the noisettes. Place the meat on a piece of foil on a broiler rack, and season lightly. If you cannot buy noisettes, bone each lamb cutlet carefully, and roll up with the eye of the meat in the center; then secure with wooden toothpicks or string.

3 Place the noisettes under a preheated moderate broiler for about 5 minutes on each side until browned and just cooked through; if you are using lamb, they can be left just slightly pink in the center – do not overcook. Alternatively, they may be fried slowly in the minimum of fat in a skillet for about 6–7 minutes on each side.

4 The rounds of bread may be fried quickly in a little heated oil for 1–2 minutes on each side, and then drained on paper towels. Otherwise simply toast the rounds on each side until golden-brown.

5 Serve each noisette on a bread croûte, and spoon the sauce over and around each one. Garnish with fresh herbs. Serve with lightly cooked fresh vegetables.

STEP 1

STEP 2

STEP 4

STEP 5

TURKISH LAMB STEW

A delicious blend of flavors with lamb, onions, and tomatoes, complete with potatoes to make a one-pot dish for two, which just needs a salad accompaniment.

SERVES 2

12 ounces lean boneless lamb
1 large or 2 small onions
1 garlic clove, crushed
¹/₂ red, yellow or green bell pepper, diced roughly
1¹/₄ cups stock
1 tbsp balsamic vinegar
2 tomatoes, peeled and roughly chopped
1¹/₂ tsp tomato paste
1 bay leaf
¹/₂ tsp dried sage
¹/₂ tsp dried dillweed
12 ounces potatoes
6–8 black olives, halved and pitted
salt and pepper

1 Cut the lamb into cubes of about ³/₄ in., discarding any excess fat or gristle. Place in a nonstick saucepan with no extra fat, and heat slowly until the fat runs and the meat begins to seal.

2 Cut the onion into 8 wedges. Add to the lamb with the garlic, and fry for an additional 3–4 minutes.

3 Add the bell pepper, stock, vinegar, tomatoes, tomato paste, bay leaf, sage, dillweed, and seasoning. Cover and simmer gently for 30 minutes.

4 Peel the potatoes, and cut into ³/₄-in. cubes. Add to the stew, and stir well. If necessary, add a little more boiling stock or water if it seems a little dry. Cover the pan again, and simmer for an additional 25–30 minutes, or until tender.

5 Add the olives, and adjust the seasoning. Simmer for an additional 5 minutes, and serve with vegetables or a salad and crusty bread.

SALAD ACCOMPANIMENT

A good salad accompaniment would be shredded white cabbage, romaine lettuce, coarsely grated carrot, diced avocado or cucumber and scallions.

CHAPTER FIVE

Desserts

Nearly everyone loves dessert, so don't be deterred from making them for only one or two people. It is probably better to make enough for two people, even if you are on your own – somehow an extra dessert is always a welcome leftover in the refrigerator, and it saves time the next day. Many desserts will keep for two or three days, so serve something different on the day in between.

Whether you are making a dessert just for yourself or are planning a special meal for two, the ideas in this chapter cover hot and cold desserts and use a wide range of flavors and ingredients. White chocolate is becoming as popular as the dark and milk kinds, and gives a new dimension to chocolate mousse; syllabub is an old favorite, but here has a subtle flavor and the color of blackcurrants from the liqueur; Alaskas, although traditionally made with ice cream in the center and covered in meringue, can instead be assembled with a delicious filling of fruits on top of the ginger cake; lime and mint give a splendid flavor and pretty appearance to cheesecake; a can of rice pudding, bananas and brown sugar are staple items ideal for an almost instant dessert; and pancakes filled and shaped into bundles with a raspberry sauce show you another delicious way of serving pancakes.

Opposite: *A dessert can consist of just fresh fruit, simply prepared. The advantage of cooking for one or two people is that using small quantities of expensive or exotic fruits is more affordable than if you are cooking for a crowd.*

STEP 2

STEP 3

STEP 5

STEP 6

LIME CHEESECAKES

These cheesecakes are flavored with lime and mint, and set on a base of crushed graham crackers mixed with chocolate.

SERVES 2

BASE:
2 tbsp butter
1 square dark chocolate
³/₄ cup crushed graham crackers

FILLING:
finely grated rind of 1 lime
¹/₃ cup creamed cottage cheese
¹/₃ cup low-fat soft cheese
1 sprig fresh mint, very finely chopped
* (optional)*
1 tsp powdered gelatin
1 tbsp lime juice
1 egg yolk
3 tbsp superfine sugar

TO DECORATE:
whipped cream
kiwi fruit slices
fresh mint sprigs

1 Grease 2 fluted, preferably loose-bottomed 4¹/₂-in. quiche or pie pans thoroughly. To make the cheesecake base, melt the butter and chocolate in a heatproof bowl over a pan of slowly simmering water, or in a microwave oven set on Full Power for about 1 minute. Stir until smooth.

2 Stir the crushed graham crackers evenly through the melted chocolate, and then press into the bottoms of the pans, leveling the top. Chill until set.

3 To make the filling, put the grated lime rind and cheeses into a bowl, and beat until smooth and evenly blended. Then beat in the mint, if using.

4 Dissolve the gelatin in the lime juice in a heatproof bowl over a saucepan of slowly simmering water, or in a microwave oven set on Full Power for about 30 seconds.

5 Beat the egg yolk and sugar together until thick and creamy, and fold through the cheese mixture, followed by the dissolved gelatin. Pour over the set cracker base and level the top, if necessary; then chill until set.

6 To serve, remove the cheesecakes carefully from the pans, and ease off the metal bottoms, if necessary. Decorate with whipped cream, slices of kiwi fruit and mint sprigs.

STEP 2

STEP 3

STEP 5

STEP 6

GINGER & APRICOT ALASKAS

No ice cream in these Alaskas, but a mixture of apples and apricots poached in orange juice enclosed in meringue.

SERVES 2

2 slices rich, dark ginger cake, about
    ³/₄ in. thick
1–2 tbsp ginger wine or rum
1 eating apple
6 no-need-to-soak dried apricots, chopped
4 tbsp orange juice or water
1 tbsp slivered almonds
2 small egg whites
¹/₃ cup superfine sugar

1 Place each slice of ginger cake on an ovenproof plate, and sprinkle with the ginger wine or rum.

2 Quarter, core, and slice the apple into a small saucepan. Add the chopped apricots and orange juice or water, and simmer slowly for about 5 minutes, or until tender.

3 Stir the almonds into the fruit, and spoon over the soaked cake, piling it up in the center.

4 Beat the egg whites until very stiff and dry, then whisk in the sugar a little at a time, making sure the meringue is stiff again before adding more sugar.

5 Either pipe or spread the meringue over the fruit and cake, making sure it is completely covered.

6 Place in a preheated oven at 400°F for 4–5 minutes until golden-brown. Serve hot.

VARIATION

A slice of vanilla, coffee, or chocolate ice cream can be placed on the fruit before adding the meringue, but this must be done at the last minute, and the Alaska must be eaten immediately after it is removed from the oven.

STEP 2

STEP 3

STEP 4

STEP 5

RASPBERRY & ORANGE PANCAKE BUNDLES

This unusual pancake is filled with a sweet cream, flavored with ginger, nuts, and apricots, and served with a raspberry and orange sauce. The surplus batter will keep in the refrigerator for a few days.

SERVES 2

BATTER:
½ cup all-purpose flour
pinch of salt
¼ tsp ground cinnamon
1 egg
generous ½ cup milk
white vegetable fat for frying

FILLING:
1½ tsp all-purpose flour, sifted
1½ tsp cornstarch
1 tbsp superfine sugar
1 egg
⅔ cup milk
¼ cup chopped nuts
¼ cup chopped no-need-to-soak dried apricots
1 piece candied or crystallized ginger, finely chopped

SAUCE:
3 tbsp raspberry preserve
1½ tbsp orange juice
finely grated rind of ¼ orange

1 To make the batter, sift the flour, salt and cinnamon into a bowl, and make a well in the center. Add the egg, and beat in the flour and milk gradually until smooth.

2 Melt a small knob of the fat in a medium skillet. When hot, pour in enough batter to cover the bottom thinly. Cook for 2 minutes until golden-brown. Then cook the other side until browned, about 1 minute. Set aside, and make a second pancake.

3 For the filling, beat together the flour, cornstarch, sugar, and egg. Heat the milk slowly in a pan, then beat 2 tablespoons of it into the flour mixture. Transfer to the saucepan, and cook slowly, stirring continuously until thick. Remove from the heat, and cover with baking parchment to prevent a skin from forming. Let cool.

4 Beat the nuts, apricots and ginger into the cooled mixture, and put a heaped tablespoonful in the center of each pancake. Gather and squeeze the edges together to make a bundle. Place in an ovenproof dish in a preheated oven at 350°F for 15–20 minutes until hot but not too brown.

5 To make the sauce, melt the preserve slowly with the orange juice, then strain. Return to a clean pan with the orange rind, and heat through. Serve with the pancakes.

PINK SYLLABUBS

The pretty pink color of this dessert is achieved by adding blackcurrant liqueur to the wine and cream before whipping.

STEP 1

SERVES 2

5 tbsp white wine
2–3 tsp blackcurrant liqueur
finely grated rind of ½ lemon or orange
1 tbsp superfine sugar
scant 1 cup heavy cream
4 ladyfingers (optional)

TO DECORATE:
fresh fruit, such as strawberries, raspberries
    or redcurrants, or pecan or walnut halves
fresh mint sprigs

1 Mix together the white wine, blackcurrant liqueur, grated lemon or orange rind, and superfine sugar in a bowl, and let rest for at least 30 minutes.

2 Add the heavy cream to the wine mixture, and whip until the mixture thickens enough to stand in soft peaks.

3 If you are using the ladyfingers, break them up roughly, and divide them between 2 glasses.

4 Put the mixture into a pastry bag fitted with a large star or plain tip, and pipe it over the ladyfingers. Alternatively, simply pour the syllabub

over the ladyfingers. Chill until ready to serve.

5 Before serving, decorate each syllabub with slices or small pieces of fresh soft fruit or nuts, and sprigs of mint.

STEP 2

NOTE

These syllabubs will keep in the refrigerator for 48 hours, so it is worth making more than you need, and keeping the extra for another day.

STEP 3

STEP 4

STEP 1

STEP 3

STEP 4

STEP 5

RICE & BANANA BRULEE

Take a can of rice pudding, flavor it with grated orange rind, candied ginger, raisins and a few sliced bananas, and top with a brown sugar glaze for a real treat.

SERVES 2

15-ounce can creamed rice pudding
grated rind of $\frac{1}{2}$ orange
2 pieces candied ginger, finely chopped
2 tsp ginger syrup from the jar
$\frac{1}{4}$ cup raisins
1–2 bananas
1–2 tsp lemon juice
4–5 tbsp brown crystal sugar

1 Empty the can of rice pudding into a bowl, and mix in the grated orange rind, ginger, ginger syrup, and raisins.

2 Cut the bananas diagonally into slices. Toss in the lemon juice, and drain. Divide between 2 individual flameproof dishes.

3 Spoon the rice mixture in an even layer over the bananas so the dishes are almost full.

4 Sprinkle an even layer of sugar over the rice in each dish.

5 Place the dishes under a preheated moderate broiler, and heat until the sugar melts, taking care the sugar does not burn.

6 Let cool until the caramel sets, then chill until ready to serve. Tap the caramel with the back of a spoon to break it.

CANNED RICE PUDDING

Canned rice pudding is very versatile, and is delicious heated with orange segments and grated apples added. Try it served cold with grated chocolate and mixed chopped nuts stirred through it.

STEP 1

STEP 2

STEP 3

STEP 4

WHITE CHOCOLATE POTS

A delicious white chocolate and rum mousse, which is only softly set and flavored with fromage frais.

SERVES 2

3 squares white chocolate
1 tbsp butter
1 tbsp rum
1 egg, separated
1 tbsp natural fromage frais

TO DECORATE:
whipped cream or natural fromage frais
fresh raspberries (optional)
fresh mint leaves

1 Break up the white chocolate, and put into a heatproof bowl with the butter. Place over a saucepan of very slowly simmering water, and heat slowly until completely melted, stirring frequently.

2 Remove the bowl from the heat, and beat in the rum, followed by the egg yolk and finally the fromage frais. Let cool.

3 Beat the egg white until very stiff and dry, and fold evenly through the white chocolate mixture.

4 Divide between 2 individual serving pots and chill until set. This mousse does not set very firmly.

5 Before serving, top each pot with a spoonful of whipped cream or fromage frais and decorate with a few raspberries and fresh mint leaves. Alternatively, sprinkle with some grated dark chocolate, or a chocolate flake bar, roughly crumbled.

VARIATION

For a variation, 1–2 tablespoons of coarsely grated chocolate can be folded through the mixture with the egg white, or dark chocolate may be used instead of white chocolate. The grated rind of $1/2$ small orange may also be added to give an orange flavoring.

MEALS FOR ONE & TWO

Whatever your situation, whether you are young or old, living alone or in a couple, retired or working full time, cooking for just one or two can present a problem. Either there is no time for shopping or elaborate cooking; or you have plenty of time, but not the inclination to make the effort to prepare a lunch or supper just for yourself. So, like many people, you need a number of quick and simple recipes that don't need elaborate ingredients, nor require you to spend hours in the kitchen, and which are interesting as well as nutritious.

The important factor is to keep the meals well balanced for a healthy diet. The recipes in this book will help you to do this, and show that you don't have to resort to junk food for convenience, or live on canned and pre-cooked food. It will also show you that it is not too much trouble to cook for just one or two people, particularly when meals can be made to stretch over two days, or even be reworked into a different dish, to serve up the following day,

BREAKFASTS

A normal breakfast for one or two will probably be based upon a bowl of cereal, followed by buttered toast perhaps spread with jam, with tea or coffee to drink. Making your breakfasts more varied doesn't have to mean a dramatic increase in preparation time, but it can make your breakfasts much more interesting, and can increase the nutritional value.

Try adding or substituting one or more of the following items to your normal breakfast, or perhaps just on weekends.

• A glass of fruit juice – orange, grapefruit, pineapple, or tomato – freshly squeezed, if possible. Not only do they taste better when freshly squeezed, but they also contain more vitamins.
• A bowl of homemade muesli with added fresh fruit, grated or sliced
• Sliced bananas, apples or soft fruit added to your normal cereal, and topped with natural yogurt or fromage frais
• Croissants or muffins, warmed in the oven, with jam or honey
• Scrambled egg: use 2 eggs per person and, if you like, add 1 ounce chopped smoked salmon pieces.
• Smoked haddock kedgeree (see below)
• Poached smoked haddock, with a poached egg on top if you like
• Poached or grilled kippers
• Broiled bacon with sausages and/or tomatoes and mushrooms
• Pancakes with maple syrup
• Spanish Omelet (see below)
• Boiled eggs

Spanish Omelet
Serves 1
2–3 slices bacon
1 small onion, finely chopped
1–2 tbsp oil
1 large boiled potato, diced
$1/3$ cup sliced mushrooms
* and/or 1–2 tomatoes, peeled and sliced*
2–3 eggs

CAKES
A piece of cake can bridge the gap between lunch and dinner, or serve as a dessert at any meal, so it is worth always having one around. Here are a few ideas:

Pound Cake
1 cup self-rising flour
$1/2$ cup all-purpose flour
$1/2$ cup butter
$1/2$ cup superfine sugar
finely grated rind of 1 lemon
2 eggs
1 tbsp lemon juice

1. Grease and line a loaf pan, about 9 × 5 in., with nonstick baking parchment.

2. Sift the flours together. Cream the fat and sugar together until very light and fluffy, and pale in color.

3. Beat in the lemon rind, then the eggs, adding 1 tablespoon of flour after each egg.

4. Fold the flours into the mixture, followed by sufficient lemon juice to give a dropping consistency.

5. Spoon the mixture into the pan and level the top. Bake in a preheated oven at 325°F for about 1 hour, until well risen and firm. A skewer inserted in the center should come out clean.

1 tbsp water
salt and pepper

1. Chop the bacon, and fry the bacon and onion in the heated oil in a skillet until sealed and lightly browned.

2. Add the potato and mushrooms and/or tomatoes, and continue cooking for 1–2 minutes.

3. Beat the eggs with the water and seasonings. Pour into the skillet, and mix lightly, then leave to settle. Cook over a low heat until set. If liked, place under a preheated moderate broiler to brown the top. Serve hot.

Smoked Haddock Kedgeree
Make as for Salmon Kedgeree on page 36, but poach 6–8 ounces smoked haddock fillet in a little water, or milk and water mixed, until tender, about 5 minutes. Then drain, remove the skin and bones, and flake roughly.

LIGHT LUNCHES AND PACKED LUNCHES
There are always days when a quick light lunch is required, or you need to pack up something to take to work, or for a trip of some sort in the car or on the train. Often these snacks will be simple, and comprise sandwiches with various fillings, sometimes incorporating bought ingredients such as pâté, cheese, canned fish, and so on. The main problem is making sure that such a meal, however small, is properly balanced, filling enough, and easy to carry if it is to be taken with you.

Salads
Salads are simple. They can easily be prepared using a wide range of fresh ingredients plus a dressing if wanted, and packed into an empty margarine carton if you are eating on the move. Buns, bread or crackers make a good accompaniment, together with a fruit or natural yogurt or some fromage frais and/or a piece of fruit, plus a fruit drink carton or can. Another salad snack that is quick to prepare is a plate of crudités eaten with a dip such as hummus or taramasalata. If teamed with a slice or two of whole wheat bread, this makes a nutritious snack.

Sandwiches
If you want to make sandwiches, then try a variety of fillings.
• Mix a can of tuna with a little mayonnaise, chopped onion, lettuce and tomato.
• On the next day, the tuna can be flavored with corn or chopped tomatoes, with a little French dressing and ketchup, topped with sliced cucumber and/or cress.
• Leftover cold meats, such as roast beef or lamb, or prepacked cold meats such as honey-roast ham or wafer-thin turkey make good fillings.
• Eggs can be used in numerous combinations, such as mixed with mayonnaise with horseradish, cress, curry powder, and mango chutney, or grated cheese and ketchup.
• Cheese can have unlimited accompaniments. Keep a selection of cheeses in the refrigerator to insure a variety of flavors.

Coffee Layer Cake
1/2 cup butter
1/2 cup superfine sugar
2 eggs
1 cup self-rising flour, sifted
*3 tsp coffee extract
  or very strong black coffee*

Butter Cream
1/4 cup butter
1 cup confectioners' sugar, sifted
*1 tsp coffee extract
  or very strong black coffee*

1. Grease and bottom line 2 round 7-in. layer pans with nonstick baking parchment.

2. Cream the fat and sugar together until light, fluffy, and pale. Beat in the eggs, following each with a spoonful of the flour. Fold in the remaining flour, followed by the coffee.

3. Divide the mixture between the pans, and level the tops. Bake in a preheated oven at 375°F for about 20 minutes, or until well risen and firm.

4. Cool in the pans for a minute or so. Then loosen the cakes, and invert on a wire rack. Leave until cold.

5. To make the butter cream, soften the butter. Then add sufficient confectioners' sugar and coffee extract to give a thick spreading consistency. Use to sandwich the cakes together, and dredge the top lightly with sifted confectioners' sugar.

Brownies
Makes 9–10
2 squares dark chocolate
1/4 cup butter
few drops of vanilla extract
3/4 cup superfine sugar
2 eggs
*1/2 cup plus 2 tbsp self-rising
    flour, sifted*
*1/4 cup chopped
    nuts or raisins*

1. Grease and line a shallow
8-in. square pan with nonstick
baking parchment.

2. Melt the chocolate and the
fat in a heatproof bowl, either
over a saucepan of slowly
simmering water, or in a
microwave oven set on Full
Power for 30–60 seconds.

3. Beat in the extract and
sugar, followed by the eggs.
Fold in the flour, followed by
the nuts or raisins, and pour
into the pan.

4. Bake in a preheated oven at
350°F for about 30 minutes, or
until risen and firm. Cool in the
pan. Cut into squares.

Wrap sandwiches in plastic wrap or foil
to keep them fresh. If you have a sweet
tooth, then add a piece of cake or a
couple of cookies.

BAKING
Baked goods are popular with everyone,
and baking is an important part of
everyday cooking, but when you are
catering for one or two, it is better to
make small cakes and smaller batches.
Choose the kinds of cake and cookie that
will keep well for several days or longer,
rather than making those which are best
eaten immediately.

For the recipes below, if you have a fan
oven, it will be a little hotter than the
conventional gas or electric oven, so
lower the suggested temperature by
about 70°F, and check the cake a few
minutes before the end of the suggested
cooking time.

When made, all cakes should be cooled
thoroughly, and then stored in an
airtight container. Empty margarine,
yogurt and fromage frais containers are
good for storing small cakes; otherwise it
is wise to buy a set of plastic containers
which will cope with all shapes and sizes.
When not in use they can be stored one
inside the other.

Here are a couple of baking recipes; for
more ideas, see the recipe columns either
side of the pages in this section.

Scones
Makes 8
2 cups self-rising flour
pinch of salt
1 1/2 tbsp superfine sugar
1/4 cup butter or margarine

1 egg, beaten
about 5 tbsp milk
1 tsp lemon juice
1/4 cup golden raisins (optional)

1. Sift the flour and salt into a bowl, and
mix in the sugar. Rub in the fat until the
mixture resembles fine bread crumbs,
then add the egg.

2. Combine the milk and lemon juice,
and add sufficient to form a fairly soft
dough, Stir in the golden raisins, if you
are using them.

3. Turn out onto a lightly floured counter
and level to a rectangle about 1 in. thick
and 4 in. wide. Cut into 8 squares.

4. Place on a lightly floured cookie sheet,
and bake in a preheated oven at 425°F
for 10–15 minutes until well risen and a
light golden-brown. Cool on a wire rack.

Flapjack Cookies
Makes 9–10
1/2 cup margarine
1/2 cup superfine or light soft brown sugar
6 tbsp light corn syrup
2/3 cup rolled oats

1. Grease or grease and line an 8-in.
shallow square cake pan with nonstick
baking parchment.

2. Cream the fat and sugar until light and
fluffy.

3. Heat the syrup until runny, and beat
into the creamed mixture, followed by
the oats. Mix thoroughly, and spoon into